ON THE BATTLEFIELD OF

Love

TYISHUA MCCOY

WAR WOUNDS

ANTHONY BRANCH

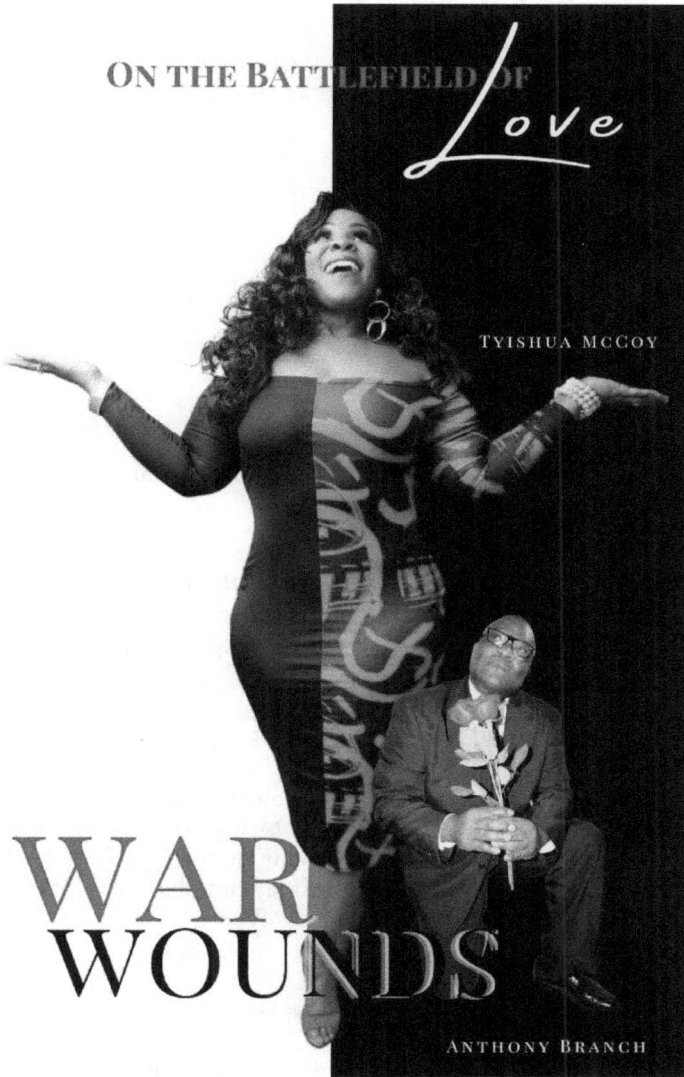

ISBN: 978-1-7341820-7-1 paperback

Photographer: Brandon Cole Photography
Author: Tyishua McCoy
Co- Author: Anthony Branch
Prologue & Poems: Jay Speight
Foreword: Annette Wooten

Cover concept and design: Danielle Ferreira

Published by: Caged Bird Publishing
www.cagedbirdpublishing.com

DEDICATION

This book is dedicated to all the individuals who didn't stop trying to get it right! You remained on the battlefield and you have been victorious! You are now reaping the benefits and enjoying the fruits of your labor. I am sure you all had a few of your own battles, and I am sure you have a few bumps and bruises to prove it! Remain vigilant and confident in your journey toward building beautiful relationships each day with each other. Continue seeking opportunities that inspire growth and change, but will still challenge you to rise to the occasion to build an even stronger foundation. While there are no perfect relationships, and surely, we are not perfect individuals, you found what was perfect for you. You took the time to find the strength in your diversity; you kicked fear in the face, shut out the doubt, and gave transparency a try. Thank you for showing us that it can be done. Please continue to lead by example and keep telling your story; trust me people are listening, watching, and wanting to know how they can find what seems to be the impossible. Hopefully, they can, and will find a few answers to their questions as they turn the page.

Tyishua McCoy

I would like to dedicate my portion of this unique book to my mother Ms. Mattie N. Branch, who raised me to the best of her abilities; and who now watches over me from Heaven.

I often tell people I got my gift of Sharing and Helping others from you, a characteristic I am most proud of; which has served me well in my adult life.

To my sister Mrs. Kim Branch-Harris, I never forget how you stepped in our mother's place, during them times when she was ill, even though you are only 3 years older than me; "A Child Yourself, Helping To Raise Children".

To Mr. James Malinchak, and Mr. Greg O'Donnell; you both have given me life changing information over the years.
You both don't know how much I needed it, at those rare times that you guys gave it to me. I appreciate you gentlemen more than you know, we are not like brothers; we are brothers.

To my former Youth Empowerment Program Vice President and "Lil Sister", Ms. LaVetta Lampley. When I was off track throughout the years, you got me back on track, in your own crazy way; that only you could.
The Friendship is real, and your Loyalty has been greatly appreciated.

To Mrs. Angela Ridle and Mr. Vince Harlston, two individuals who are the "Voices Of Reason" for me here in Northwest Indiana.

To my San Antonio Texas Family, Ms. Melissa Blue and Ms. Janice Steele-McMillan; Thank You both for your words of wisdom and prayer.

~Anthony Branch

PROLOGUE

Real Love?

My girl cheated when we almost got married; the fact I'm still
single and getting older is getting scary.
Cause, the dating scene ain't always what it seems.
I'm starting to think love only exists in our dreams.
Do you really know what it means to love unconditionally?
It has nothing to do with what someone can do for me...

Not even close.
For better or for worse rather I'm rich or I'm broke.
My love life going in circles like wheels on some spokes.
When I think I'm winning I'm LeBron in Cleveland I just choke.
Every time I had hope I end up being left broken hearted.
Then I meet someone new and I'm back where I started.
Is this what it's supposed to feel like?

Are my senses just numb or maybe emotionally retarded?
Cause nothing is going the way it's supposed to be, and women
don't listen these days not even destiny...

Sometimes I just want to quit, you must need a vacation cause
every day you just trip. I feel my self-starting to slip back to who I

used to be in my player stage.

Cause nobody seems to be sincere it seems now a days...

If we afraid of getting hurt, then who's keeping it real, you holding
all the cards but too scared to deal.

I meet a lot of women and I'm still, a lonely man, I know that's
hard to understand from the outside looking in.

My hands are tied, I'll just try to do the best I can...

Maybe one day I'll get my chance…

My heart hurts but I'm far from a broken man.

The key witness to who killed Cupid ready to take the stand.

Hand on the bible, the other in the sky, promising not to lie
keeping my eyes on prize...

Hoping to find Real Love before I die but if I don't, it won't be
because I never tried.

~Jay Speight

ACKNOWLEDGEMENTS

I would first like to give an honor to God for giving me the vision and the countless experiences to meet the needs of so many that have been searching for something that will speak to them concerning knowledge of self, self-care, and relationships in such a manner, that it can be understood in the most simplistic way. Each page and thought-provoking sentence will assist in lighting a path that will guide you carefully through each decision that you will make moving forward.

Thank you to my husband, Mr. Kevin McCoy for your patience, for listening and supporting me through this project. I pray that we will continue to be a light and blueprint collectively and individually to each other as well as for others throughout our lifetime of love and relationship. I would like to thank my mother, Brenda L. King for her persistence in instilling confidence, courage, and strength in me before her passing. She showed me how a woman is supposed to conduct herself and treat others even when you are not favored in their eyes. To my Grandparents Mr. Austin King and Mrs. Evelyn King, I would like to thank them for showing me what a marriage ordained by God looks like. I appreciate the 47 years of love and respect you gave each other before you both passed.

I would like to give a huge thank you to the following for all the support, blood, sweat and tears from those that contributed to this project, Ms. Danielle Ferreira CEO, of Caged Bird Publishing, for believing in this project from day one. I truly appreciate the unbelievable skill, talent and creativity you pour into your clients and now family! To Mr. Johnnie Blaze and Annette Parker, your insight and transparency adds just the right amount of seasoning to this book that will lead readers to your next literary master-pieces. To my Co-Author, Mr. Anthony Branch, thank you for taking a giant leap of faith to blindly do this joint venture with me. Your knowledge and wisdom will surely be found and warranted by many. Thank you, Ms. Shelia Beale, for your willingness to keep us on track and in the know at all times. Thank you for your many prayers and planning to make sure we remained grounded and focused. I give a gigantic thank you to every single person that I ever had a conversation with, if we ever shed tears, some laughter, a smile, an argument, or ever had a difference of opinion, I sincerely thank you. Each of you have, and will continue to help me to mature, change and grow in a positive and productive way. Because of you, I know I have a better sense of self, and how to respond to others no matter the situation or circumstance. Be responsible for your actions, for they may, or may not cause others to react negatively or differently!

~ Tyishua McCoy

I would like to Acknowledge God, for giving me the Wisdom I have obtained; by surviving the tragedies I had in my life.

To my "Inner Circle" in Northwest Indiana, thank you all for believing in me, and always wanting the best for me daily.

To Mrs. Tyishua McCoy, Ms. Shelia Beale, and Ms. Danielle Ferreira; this book was not possible without you all. You all are innovative and different, in your own little ways; and that's why you are all very unique.

To my mentor and dear friend Mr. James Malinchak, you have taught me so much over the years, and you are always a phone call away, if I ever need your advice or wisdom sir. I Sincerely Thank You All.

~ Anthony Branch

CONTENT

FOREWORD

Every thought begins with the planting of a seed and hence, when watered, a result blossoms, whether a positive manifestation or a negative one. Upon an encounter with the opposite sex, there are those occasions when an attraction develops thereby producing a continuous "thought" of that individual. A mutual reaction from the one admired is now the catalyst which ignites the flames of a blooming romance.

Data of one another is collected and stored via communication whether by phone calls, text messages or simply by arranging a date and looking in the eyes of the object of your desire. Questions are posed as a quest to "get to know" the one whom you are now attracted to. Answers are provided, some true and some not so true as the "best foot forward" mentality guides the quest to be liked or ultimately loved. Stories are shared which enhances the attraction along with playful anecdotes as an attempt to present another side of oneself. Usually, the first date determines whether these individuals will continue to pursue one another, or a deal-breaker has brought it to a conclusion.

There is always a motivation behind every action or decision and that which is of a selfish nature is oftentimes hidden and not discovered until months or years later. These individuals may lie and deceive the one who may be in love with love and willing to settle for any treatment to avoid loneliness, an image, or an empty bed. Low self-esteem and a loathing of a "single-self" attracts those ready to acquire a new victim.

Why is it that some deny the enhancement of themselves and pour every fiber of their being into one who is not deserving? Why it is that ill behavior is forgiven only to place you in a repeated cycle of dishonor and disrespect?

We all may have heard of true love stories; two people meet, decide to date, and eventually end up married! Honesty, commitment, and love are the driving forces with no hidden agendas. A sincere acceptance, a dedicated mind and heart is the catalyst to this ideal scenario.

As you the reader, delves into the masterpiece, *"War Wounds, on the Battlefield of Love"* written by Author, Tyishua McCoy and Co Author, Anthony Branch, glimpses of oneself may be captured. You will experience the heart of Tyishua McCoy as she guides, advises and encourage readers. Passionate about the unfathomable essence of love, this read will force you to take a deep look at what drives your motivation on dating, love, sex, and commitment. You will experience the personal and objective views of Mr. Anthony Branch, as he gives it to you from one man's point-of-view.

This book, is a must read for the world in which we live today with a no holds barred approach; they tell it like it is! Tyishua McCoy's heart is the driving force behind the messages, sharing lessons and truths afforded to them in the throes of love. *"War Wounds, on the Battlefield of Love"* is thought provoking, inspiring and a tutor which will turn your seeds into a manifestation of love and NOT a battleground.

~ Annette Wooten

Chapter 1

Talk is Cheap

By: Tyishua McCoy

Yes, we have all heard the saying "Talk is cheap". I am so sure, you have said it a time or two when referring to relationships. As men and women, we all have a tendency to walk right into a situation that will have you lost, mad, disappointed and utterly confused. I want to get right to the point. I am not going to use a lot of big fancy words, or any famous quotes, well maybe a few, but I'm definitely not going to beat around the bush. I'm going to give it to you straight with no chaser!

When you dive into any conversation with someone who you

are potentially looking at as a significant other, maybe a new bae or boo, and if you are feeling real lucky, like you have hit the jackpot, you may have landed a husband or a wife! There are three major situations you should avoid at all costs:

Individuals who are currently married, separated or fresh out of a relationship! I call these the Transition Positions or (TP's). When you are in a TP situation, you just need to sit down and get your thoughts together, because you are sure to make more mistakes moving forward too quickly or too soon, and I mean far more than you did in the previous relationship you just came out of. Your heart and mind are still processing the hurt, pain or trauma from the previous situation. There is no way you are ready to make any sure moves, or decisions concerning a relationship.

Most, if not all the choices you make will be irrational, emotional, and worst of all, physical. Most of you will be setting yourselves up for an epic fail, and it will be all on you! You will have no one to blame but yourself.

If your mind is all over the place, your body will follow. You keep thinking "I need to get over him or her as quickly as possible". Trust me a new "Any-Body" is not the answer!

You will only be setting yourself up for more heartache and pain, and may be even some mid-life drama. This is a sure-fire way to ignite the biggest bomb in your life to explode leaving bits and pieces of you all over the place, in other words, BROKEN!

Men and women process pain very differently. Most men are physical, visual and are able to easily disconnect. They have short attention spans and get bored quickly. If it looks good, feels good, smells good, then it's all good. While most women are more mentally and emotionally present, they also have the tendency to lead more with their hearts. A woman's follow-through to move to the next phase in a relationship is based on most men's actions, what he may say, and what timeframe he may do it in.

Men complain about women either talking too much, not listening enough, or not understanding their needs. Women complain about men either not being mentally and emotionally supportive, or not being expressive about their feelings, or not attentive or affectionate enough.

First, let me say this, do not allow yourself to be suckered in by "short term" situations that will have you thinking it could possibly end up with you in a relationship. No matter how handsome, pretty, or good the sex is, these things should not be guiding you down the relationship path.

Please let me be clear, yes, we all want someone that we will be attracted to, but if that is the driving force to meet your mate, it will be short lived, and your problems will be greater than all the lakes in Michigan!

Your physical attributes should not be the focus for you or the individual you are seeking interest in, especially when you have so many other great qualities within. Allow those qualities to reflect just as much as the outward attraction. Now, I am not speaking for every man or woman in this book, however I want to give you all an opportunity to look and think differently about certain situations that you have all tried, and yet they have all failed. Think for a moment, what was leading you to pursue that individual?

There is someone out there for every type of person but you should not go out there trying to be every type of person. Be who you are, if you are in a TP and you are trying to change your situation by seeking self-improvement, do not involve yourself with anyone. You are in a transitional state!

If you used to be a serial dater, or a pathological liar, dealing with depression, or any type of substance abuse, or the death of a significant other or spouse, even divorce is considered a life altering situation, and emotions can clash with your mental health and cause serious instability within your life. Bringing in another individual while dealing with any of those issues is a recipe for disaster. I give you this piece of information for those that are out there and still single, I know the challenges you face, and they will make you feel frustrated and discouraged.

Although you may feel like you are spinning out of control, the TP requires patience. This is also the period you learn to love yourself a little more. The good, the bad, and the ugly parts of you will be revealed if you trust the process.

I know there are people out here who are going a 100 miles per hour to jump into bed with someone, but yet, will do 10 miles per hour when entertaining a relationship…BACKWARDS! The greatest time that should be taken is you getting to know you! Clean up the mess you made or what you allowed others to make in your life. If you are focused on that, you will be in tune with the individual that is meant for you.

If you try to entertain any type of relationship while you are in the Transition Position or (TP), you may miss that opportunity for real love in a lasting relationship. Situations that do not serve a purpose in your life may hinder you from allowing that special someone of substance to come into your life. You don't have to be religious or spiritual to know that words have power, and if you are that man or woman who says "relationships are too hard", you may have even said "I'm never getting married" or "I'm not the marrying kind" or "it's not my thing", and usually, those are the first ones to say "I do". Do know, you are speaking all manners of doubt into your life when you put these things in the atmosphere, and if this is truly how you feel and what you want, you don't have to speak it; just be about that life, but don't try to pull others into your "wet cement" way of thinking! Most, if not all women, want a man who is decisive and clear about his needs, wants and desires.

Now ladies, stop trying to read between the lines, and listen to what men are saying and don't be so caught up in the bedroom. And don't get mad or bent out of shape because you missed it when he said "He likes to chill by himself" of course, until he needs something or someone warm to lie next to, to have a need fulfilled.

Ladies, if you know you need and want more out of him, or the relationship, why are you even entertaining the conversation with this individual. Men, why go through the motions of setting her up for the fall.

We cannot think that if we use the same old failed ideas concerning relationships, we can expect a different result. The mind will need to be redesigned to think about the situations that will drive us into successful relationships, not the ones that will cause heartache and disappointment, yet we set ourselves up to receive it. Not all situations are our fault; however, whatever contributions good or bad that you add can make or break a situation.

Some buy into the word "compromise". I say this because, this is usually the reason given when a relationship goes south. He or she didn't want to "compromise". Do you even know the true meaning or definition of the word? Do you use it more so to try to get your way or manipulate a situation? Is it your way to reason with yourself or with an idea you know shouldn't even be suggested or entertained in the first place?

Let me just give you an idea or illustration of how someone chooses to compromise in a simple situation:

The scenario is, you have been talking to someone for a little over two weeks. Every day the conversations have been very pleasant, intriguing and informative. You both have disclosed that you are a straight forward type of individual, and you don't play games. You know what you want and need in a relationship. Now you have both set a time to meet up for lunch, dinner, coffee or just drinks. You have both agreed on a place and time to meet. Remember, I said all conversations you have had up until this point have been enjoyable, pleasant and informative. You arrive on time even early and the other party hasn't arrived yet, and 15 minutes have passed, 30 minutes have passed, no call or text as to why they're late. You called and there is no answer or reply to your text. You continued to wait; you even ate dinner, and had a drink. After 45 minutes, they arrived. You are boiling inside, and because they are so handsome, smelling Irish Spring clean, with a smile like the Sun, and built Ford tough, or she got this Beyoncé body and booty, the twins on her chest looking just right, and what most of you will do is, give into all these dynamics and accept the apology with no explanation concerning the tardiness, and total disregard for your time! I am not saying all women or men buy into these situations, I am just looking at all the facts; you talked for two weeks, shared intimate details about wants and needs of a relationship. You gave your deal-breakers and deal-makers, you even spoke on your pet peeves, one of them being not being punctual and not communicating effectively. What some people do is test you to see if you are who you say you are, or if you are this version of something you made up in your head, or are you trying to be something that you not ready to be? The biggie; the test to see what they can get away with.

If you were bothered by the situation, but too distracted by the physical, you will continue to allow these situations to grow into something very toxic and out of control. You should have communicated at that very moment how you felt. It's your first-time meeting, and you say you don't want to make any waves; well, a flood is what you will endure if you start compromising your respect, time and worth now.

You should communicate with tact and understanding, and the individual would have to consider your feelings. And, if at that moment they cannot, then you are setting yourself up for more such situations to come if you move forward with this situation.

Someone who is not considerate of your time will surely waste it, in every sense of the phrase. The battles that we constantly fight are not with each other, it is with ourselves, and with who we are struggling to become. The fight within yourself is definitely a force to be reckoned with.

If you know you have challenges with being honest, faithful, kind, loving, affectionate or respectful, why would you try your hand at a relationship? Trying to incorporate someone in your life while you are struggling with these bad habits or inconsistent behaviors, will be a situation full of arguments, disagreements, and unfulfilled compromises. If you choose to move forward with someone and you still possess these characteristics, how can you possibly think that your motives will be sincere? Would you allow someone who struggles with the same issues into your life?

You have to have a mindset that desires change! You have to be willing to express and be clear about your wants and needs concerning relationships.

If you meet someone and you see they're happy, and life is beautiful for them, they are in a good place, mentally, emotionally and spiritually, and I don't mean they are on some false sense of reality trip, I mean they are in tune with who they are, then they have created balance within. Unlike some who experience daily mood swings, or don't know who they want to be, or what they want to do from one day to the next, unable to multi-task life's ups and downs, and no general knowledge on how to cope. Everyday seems like a struggle just to be at peace.

Most individuals want to have peace of mind and to be able to get along in life without everyday seeming like a dark highway, where you can't see what's ahead of you, and no clue of where you are going. You just feel lost. The last thing you need to do is pull someone into your world, when you yourself have no clue of what is going on. Don't darken someone else's world with your confusion or chaos. We all need someone to talk to. If you have no friends or family that you trust with giving you sound advice or guidance concerning your innermost thoughts due to fear of judgement or criticism, seek some type of professional therapy. Your mental health is very important! When you are seeking clarity, sometimes advice from friends or family can be very damaging, especially, when you are already indecisive. In some instances, they may not want to tell you the truth about yourself. If you know, you have not made good choices in the past, talk to people who are already where you want to be! Not just in relationships, but in life, period!

You don't know what it may have taken for an individual to get to the place of peace that they are in, or what obstacles they had to overcome, and then you met someone, and they want and need the same in their life, and here you come; on purpose misrepresenting yourself to them.

Before you utter one hello, think about the things you know, and in fact, struggle with; improve in those areas first. Don't just try…DO IT! If you wanted a new pair of shoes you didn't try to buy them, you either did or you didn't. Sometimes we talk so much, that we talk ourselves right out of what we want and need. Second-guessing yourself only breaks down your mental ability to think confidently. The words "If and Try" handicaps us. They are just comfortable words we use that will give us an excuse or an easy way out if we fail.

Look, we are not perfect! We all will make mistakes and the less you make, shows your progress. You are no longer trying, you are following through, and you are now giving yourself the time, proper self-care, and investment needed to be a better version of yourself.

Chapter 2

The Truth Hurts So Good

By: Tyishua McCoy

You are out with your friends at a small gathering where most of the people that are attending are married couples, or out with a significant other. They are holding hands, looking deep into each other's eyes, having pleasant conversations and enjoying each other's presence. And when they leave, it's with the one they love, not someone they just met for the moment. You feel like the odd-ball-out, because your conversations can't or may not relate, or it appears as if you are flirting or trying to entice someone with unwanted discussions.

You take a hard look around and see you are single as a Pringle! You now start a conversation in your head, you begin to run off all the wonderful things about yourself, I'm a Boss, not bad looking, as a matter fact; I'm fly, handsome, or beautiful, smart, I got plenty to offer, they are crazy not to get with this.

These should not be the things that inspire you to want a relationship, or for someone to want you. These attributes will be the very things that will have you appearing desperate. Yes, you may be attractive but what's up with your values, morals, and mindset. Now those will be the real show-stopper for someone who truly desires something of substance.

I would like to speak to my ladies for a moment. If someone is only interested in you because, you have long hair, pretty feet, or for the size of your posterior, or your outward beauty, that will surely attract them, but only for a moment, along with every other woman out here that may possess the same things!

Your authentic self will win every single time! There is something about you that nobody else can duplicate; the one or many things that will separate you from every other person. There is someone out here that will love it to life! You may not even know what that may be, but have fun discovering it by being yourself daily. Please keep this in mind, don't expect others to love the things you love about yourself, someone else may not like, love or even find those things attractive.

Where are all my "people pleasers" at? Yes, the ones who think because they hold back giving someone a piece of their mind or possess a certain amount of tact, or because they start and end every sentence with, yes, please and thank you, or because they are the first to apologize. If you know this is not who you really are, then please stop giving people this false sense of who you are trying to be! I get it. We all need to be respectful and polite, but not uptight!

I see so many men and women go so far outside of themselves to see what they can catch by being something they are not. I have men and women, who now want to be gym rats. You look in the mirror and you see you have a little bit more in the middle, so you now force conversations about working out, as if they are really interested in your workout routine. If you want to maintain your health wonderful, then do that, but no one wants to hear about all the healthy foods you probably just started eating yesterday, or how long you stayed on the treadmill or elliptical machine at the Planet Fitness!

And ladies, if you know you like to wear make-up because you like it, then wear it! Just because a man says, you don't need it, that should not be the end all to your make-up days, you both just met; will he even be around the next 30 days? Just say thank you for the compliment as you sit there with your face looking flawless as that beautiful bronzer is highlighting those cheekbones!

The same goes for your hair. If you are natural, great! Please don't shame other women because they like to wear weave, extensions or wigs. The truth is some women need it! To all my men out there who ridicule or look down at women who wear make-up, wigs, weaves or extensions, just date and marry what you want. No need for extra conversation concerning your reasons as why it is not your thing! Why meet a woman who wears make-up and then try to convince her she doesn't need it? Gentlemen, what if you are bald, and she talks to you about using some hair loss products, or if your teeth are not bright white and she tells you, you have a great smile but your teeth could be whiter. Trust me; that "you don't need make-up" line does not always come across as a compliment.

And let us not forget our ladies who add to their assets. Adding some boobies or booty, makes for a great milkshake to bring all the boys to the yard! I just hope that you are doing all of this for you, and not just to get a man or the added attention from men.

Please understand I am not referring to all women or men, however, I am speaking to the group who is doing this to please others. Once you come to the realization as to why you do what you do, your mind will be stress free from people pleasing. Your happiness starts with you! The quicker you recognize that, you will attract what you want and need. Your mind will be clearer to see what is approaching you. You will not have to wonder whether that person is being authentic or sincere in their approach, or if it's a fabricated version of the real thing, or a representative.

If you continue to allow your inadequacies to dictate, who you are and what you need, you will settle for anything that comes your way and feels comfortable and easy. You ask, "Shouldn't I want someone who loves me for me?" Yes, of course. But the real question is, do you love you for you? Are you being the best true self you can be, or are you doing just enough to get by, to just pass for being great?

When do you start changing your approach about relationships into a positive and progressive mindset? You should want to reshape your thinking as you grow and change for the better. You have to start the process now in order to get a handle on it. You need to discover what is deep inside, and what is holding you back from having the loving, caring, and beautiful relationship you claim you deserve and want.

Where are all my "deep thinkers" at? I want to challenge you today to do a simple task. This is an assignment to help with seeing how consistent you are in your daily living. You will take on a very simple task, you can choose what it should be, and do it for three days. I don't care what it is! If it's just putting a penny away in a jar beside your bed at the same time each day every night, do it. Then do it for three more days until you have completed this task for 21 days. Do it purposely, consistently and consciously. Develop an attitude to do something intentionally, until it becomes a habit. Think of all the unhealthy habits you have accomplished and consistently done without even trying. Redesign your mind to do something that will help you, not hinder you.

This concept is new to some, but old to many! My question is, if you know about it, why haven't you tried it? What harm will it do, or have done to try something new. Again, you have to redesign your mind from the foolish ways you used to think. Yes, I am sure there is someone reading this now, and saying that isn't going to work for me. Well, my love, you are not ready for change or growth because in order for anything to work, it has to be done intentionally, deliberately and with purpose.

We allow so many things to deter us from the very things we think we can't have. There are no perfect relationships! I mean what is the fun in that. Looking past a person's faults and flaws is easy when they are so in tune with who you are and doing all the right things.

The energy and the chemistry you are bringing to the relationship is what could potentially keep you together. But, what about the times they are not doing what you like, they make you mad, or even have you questioning the relationship. What then? The key is consistency! If you are doing enough of the good stuff, the storm will only look like rain. We have all heard the saying "the good should outweigh the bad".

This is part reason why a few marriages do last. They had a whole lot of awesome and amazing moments, so when the big wave came it did not feel like a Tsunami.

Whether you want it or not, change is inevitable. You are supposed to change for the better in all relationships, personal, professional, and public. If you have entertained more than one relationship in your lifetime, you should have taken something away that will help you, not hinder you into the next step or phase of your life. They should have been used as teachable moments. However, if you continue with the same old damaging patterns that left you or the last person emotionally unfulfilled, then you need to take a step back from dating until you get yourself together, I mean **REALLY** together! If you only just want sex or the occasional hook-up from time to time, then do it with people that want the same, and have the same mindset concerning that type of situation. How do you find those types of people, you ask? How about be honest in your conversations, and the time that you are requesting from them.

Those individuals will know and understand the repercussions concerning the outcome. Trust me; no matter how unhealthy the situation, you are not the only one out here who wants to entertain that madness.

Just remember this, if you decide to move forward with this type of foolishness with someone who does not know that these are your intentions, you will leave that person very confused about what it is that you want, and you may even cause serious emotional and mental harm to those individuals.

Honestly, the best thing to do is, shut down any kind of sexual contact with anyone when you are going through this phase of your life. Any doubts that you may have about yourself or relationship will make for a mess and breed unwanted drama.

Also, be truthful about where your head is during this phase in your life, and be brutally honest. The freedom in letting someone know that you cannot possibly entertain a relationship or any kind of friendship right now, sets you up to gain so much respect not just from the other individual, but for yourself. I mean, honestly do you really need another male or female friend in your life? You do not need a rolodex of men or women to call when the first or third person did not answer your call, or respond to your text. SIT YO ASS DOWN SOMEWHERE!

Casual encounters are just that, casual. There is no safety or security in a relationship that is based on convenient, meaningless, unfulfilled sexual acts. I hear you out there mumbling, "But I got needs"! I understand that there are sexual needs but ask yourself should you have to sacrifice being unfulfilled for a temporary sexual need, or for that matter, should someone else?

If we all carefully take a deeper approach to what sex really cultivates, some of you would truly think twice before laying on your back, then again there are some who will let this go in one ear and right out the other, but hopefully most of you will listen and understand the dynamics.

Sex is not just sex no matter how you slice or dice it. It is called intercourse for a reason; anything you enter into, something is going to change mentally, emotionally, physically, spiritually and even financially. Sex can and will change all those dynamics. No one is exempt. All of us have been, or will be affected one way or another.

If you are reckless with sex, it will be reckless with you. Do you really need me to break it down for you? Ok, let us start with those good ole STD's, and yes there are still a few out there you can't get rid of with a shot or a pill, also unwanted pregnancies. Children are being born to parents who are mentally, emotionally or financially not ready. Please let us not forget if you have multi-partners that do not know about each other, adding pain, hurt and embarrassment that could be caused in marriages or even relationships where you thought you were the only one.

If you are gentle and respect sex, it will be gentle and respect you. We have a moral obligation and responsibility to ourselves, and others to set an example. Certain behaviors you exhibit, will surely affect your integrity. Whether you know it or not, there is someone, somewhere that follows you, and hangs on your every word. You do not have to be famous or a celebrity to have such people in your circle of associates. Some people will look to you on a positive level, others on a negative level.

You truly have to be careful when making certain moves, especially if you have children. Not all but most children will follow in the footsteps of their parents, peers, or the persons that have the most or heaviest influence on them.

Involving yourself in casual encounters to feel wanted and desired, if only for a few moments, can lead to depression, self-esteem issues, and possibly, you could become desensitized to the wants and needs of a meaningful relationship.

Somehow, we rationalize the truth about how others see us. You may think you are this great and wonderful man or woman. But how do you identify with those who you have had relationships with in the past or even currently?

Remember, they had a chance to see your inner core, the raw essence of who you really are, even if you did not share your entire life with them. For a moment, you were vulnerable and you let your guard down. You may not even remember every conversation, or sexual encounter, but I bet, in the midst of those walls coming down, the person you were with may remember those intimate details, along with every word, every shine in your eye, to each breath that you took!

Some men and women need sex or some type of validation in order to feel good about themselves. This is how they deflect from the realities of life. No one wants to really deal with his or her shortcomings. Instead, we sometimes go on doggie paddling, when we could be floating.

When I say floating, I am not speaking of having a "go with the flow" mentality, I am asking you to take time out to "smell the roses" sometimes. Slowdown, not for work, kids, friends, pets, or house-work, but for YOU!

Sometimes we are moving so fast, we miss some very important things. I'm speaking of little opportunities we may have missed that we should have paid closer attention to, things we should have listened to a little more carefully, maybe something we should have read, or even people who we may have encountered for reasons other than a simple conversation in the grocery store line, or the office water cooler.

It's just so disheartening that some folks, would rather subject themselves to drama, foolishness, gossip, and or petty innuendos. And I am finding more men are allowing themselves to be pulled into these types of matters. Not saying these should mainly be issues concerning women, I wish as women, we would not entertain them either, but it has been said that men gossip more than women, and get in their feelings and are just as petty, if not more than women as well.

I am just going to come right out and say it, *"men, your slips are showing"*! Gentlemen, this is not an attractive quality. Now men, I am in no way saying that you do not have feelings, and/or that you should not express them if and, when you are hurt, or feel disrespected. Those matters should definitely be handled immediately. However, you should be cognizant of what you say and what you do when it comes to certain matters dealing with women.

Some of the things you do in response when you are mad or upset with your girlfriend, wife or significant other may come across as a little feminine, and could very well become a turn-off for many women. As the saying goes, *"Girl you can't do what a man do, and still be a Lady"*, well men, the same goes for you too, you can't do what a woman do, and still think you will be looked at as being the "MAN" or manly.

Now ladies, I want to speak to you just for a moment, because I do not ever want you to feel slighted in the least. We cannot and should not emasculate a man in public or private! There is always a classy way to do everything. If you are a woman who is educated, cultured and financially straight, you should in no way use that to put him down or make him or anyone feel less than. If you are seeking a man, and you wish for him to have acquired the same achievements as you, there is nothing wrong with that. Just remember there are some great blue-collar men out there, and they are just as educated with a street degree, cultured, financially straight, and very willing and able to treat you the way you deserve to be treated and loved!

Cars, big bank accounts, houses, prestigious jobs or titles, do not make an individual; it just shows us where their focus lies or may have been for a period in time. Statistics show that more women are independent by force not by choice, so we all understand the "I am woman, hear me roar" mentality. What most women fail to realize is, this way of thinking does not help when you are trying to achieve a relationship with substance. No one will ever measure up to you, if you feel you are over and above a man. Most men desire a woman who acts and carries herself like a lady, not too opinionated, soft with her words, strong not masculine; however, she is able to articulate her wants, needs and feelings, as well as stand up for herself, a little seductive, and sensual with her touch. You may possess all of these qualities, and now you are asking yourself, why and how is it, I am missing the mark when it comes to relationships? You must have balance, not just with one, but with all the qualities you bring to the table.

There are quite a few men out there, who love a smart woman. They are even turned on by the thought of having one in their lives. If you are dating, and a man has expressed this is a quality he adores about you, or women in general, this is not the time to start blurting off all your achievements, awards and degrees. Smart does not necessarily equate to or mean you are intelligent, or vice versa.

Don't be so eager to please, or fit into a box that may not be made for you. You may not even be his idea of smart. He may need or want a woman that may be book smart, street smart, financially smart, or spiritually smart. Intelligence comes in many different shapes, sizes and colors, so be very careful when having those conversations.

Chapter 3

Inspiration vs. Desperation

By: Tyishua McCoy

I believe there is someone out there for everyone. However, you do not have to be with everyone to find that someone! Ask yourself do you have standards, or do you have expectations? What are your standards or expectations? Are you an example of them? Are you representing what it is you stand for, expect, or need in the type of relationship that you desire?

The math is very simple ladies and gentlemen, if you are out there serial dating, sleeping with any and everything, you lying through your teeth about the little things, God forbid what big stuff you may be lying about. You are financially jacked up because you broke on another level, you bought a car that you may as well be living in, because you pay more than rent or mortgage to drive it, you buying clothes that are dry clean only, when you don't even own a washer and dryer.

Who are you? What are you doing? Your priorities are all out of sorts, and you are spinning out of control and you don't even know it, or you may know it, and you chose to stay in the chaos because you have lived this life for so long, you are quite comfortable content and have become immune to it.

The truth is, there are so many that are comfortable in the wrong way of doing things, while others, may have been innocently taught this way of life. You may have seen your parents, or whoever raised you, do these same things and live this same life. And it looked cool and was very convenient and easy. Our backgrounds, and how we were raised, has significant bearing on how we respond and do just about everything in life, including relationships.

I will get a little personal for a moment. I was raised by a single mother, and she had relationships while I was growing up, however it was my Grandparents' marriage that inspired me to want a relationship that would hopefully lead to marriage! Throughout my years as a young girl to becoming an adult, I wanted what I saw between my grandparents. The love, loyalty, respect they gave each other was undeniable. My grandfather didn't care who you were, even his own children couldn't disrespect his wife or bring a hurtful tear to her eye. The protection was that of a King to his Queen. My grandfather's name was Mr. Austin King II and he was as strong as the name. He stood 6 foot 5 inches; he filled a room with his presence and his voice. He would come in the house, and from the depths of his soul, he would say HELLO IN THIS HERE HOUSE! When he entered, he would remove his hat, and he greeted his wife with the sweetest kiss! The atmosphere would change, and everyone spoke back or gave a hug. We all would sit up straight, we got quiet, and whoever was in his favorite chair, you got up and moved to the floor or to another chair in the room. It was time to settle down and be peaceful. My grandmother made sure no one bothered him, as he sat to recoup and relax from a hard day's work. You watched what he watched on TV, if you didn't like it, you went outside or to your room, but it definitely was not up for debate. Dinner was cooked and no one ate until he came home and yes, the first plate was to my grandfather. His food and drink was brought to him on a tray, and it was served and received with such humility and respect, because it was prepared with love.

He was my protector, my hero, and he gave the best hugs. When he picked me up, I felt like I could touch the clouds. He was the closest thing I had as a representative of a father. He would come home from work just about the same time every day, and very rarely did I see my grandfather come in all hours of the night. He took care of the home and whatever repairs were needed, if he couldn't fix it, he wasn't so prideful that he couldn't call someone to repair it. My grandmother was the caretaker of the inside of the home. She decorated the house with her own unique style, we had designated days and times to clean and dust the house whenever all the grandkids were there, and she also had a garden in the back yard where she grew tomatoes, cucumbers, lettuce, corn, collard greens and string beans, and I can't forget the peach tree. The memories as I write this are so beautiful. She knew her role, and so did my grandfather. Now, neither one of them had a role-model, blue-print, or an example of what to do as far as how to treat each other or how a man should treat a woman, or how a woman should treat a man! My grandmother was the mother in the household and took care of her brothers and sisters, and my Granddad's father left his mother when he turned 18 years old. So how did they last 47 years? My grandmother's blueprint of marriage was based on the principles in the Bible. She knew she was this virtuous God-fearing woman, though she was beautiful, she needed a man who would value and recognized those characteristics in her. Even though they fulfilled each other's needs, they still had their issues, ups, downs, hills and valleys. My grandmother said they disagreed behind closed doors. However, my grandmother did disclose that there were a couple times she threw a few Campbell soup cans at him, no my grandfather was not a violent man, no he didn't fight back, he just ducked! He knew when he was in the wrong, and took his medicine like a man. My grandmother just had her own way of solving issues to get his attention so that he knew she was serious about whatever issues needed to be resolved at that time. Again, I never saw this behavior from either one of them; of course this was in their young love days. I guess the good outweighed any of the offenses he may have committed, because they were married 47 years before my grandfather passed away. My Grandmother never remarried or entertained another man. In my Grandmother's words, "there will never be another Junior King".

Now, I am telling a story that is a specific part of my childhood, because this was my blueprint for relationships and family. My grandparents may not have had an example to live by, because they chose to be what they needed to be in the marriage; there were standards and expectations with the days of old relationships as well. They chose to be what was good for them, and what they both wanted from and for each other. When someone wants something completely different from the other individual in the relationship and those things have not or, had not, been discussed before the relationship or marriage started, it will surely deteriorate.

I learned how to conduct myself as a young lady who was

developing into a young woman from watching and listening to my mother, grandmother and the women in my family. I would one day have my own husband and family to take care of. I viewed how a man is supposed to treat a woman, and how and when he was to provide for her and his family. There was no boyfriend and girlfriend living situations encouraged in our family. You couldn't and wouldn't sleep over with anyone in their home if you were not husband and wife. These were not expectations, these were standards!

If anyone in our family chose that particular type of situation to be in, in other words (Shacking), as our elders would say, that was because they chose to settle for that idea of a relationship not because it was observed, or taught.

I learned everything growing up from watching and listening to what heavily influenced me, from how to cook, even down to how to discipline and rear my children, all came from this setting. This way of life indeed inspired me to want a beautiful, healthy, fulfilling marriage. This is where it all comes together or falls apart! If you come from a similar background as I did, you forget a few important factors as you are choosing your mate. If you need specifics in your relationship parallel to your upbringing, then you need to do your homework before you even go to dinner or to bed! However, in this day and time people are super lazy, especially some women. Statistically, it's more women than men in this day and time, and women seem to be in competition, either for someone else's man or husband, or for a man that will probably not even give you a fulfilling friendship, yet less, a relationship or marriage. Some women would rather have half a man, than no man at all.

We as women should not become so desperate or wrapped up in looks, cars and bank accounts, that we tuck all the red flags away and hope and pray they don't resurface, or you think if you are so super gorgeous and got the good-good in the bedroom, that you can turn him into this figment of your imagination. Men, this goes for you too, those of you who think you are bedroom gurus, and do the same things and will try to turn that into a relationship without commitment. Granted, there is a small percentage of cases that may work in the favor of the many individuals that choose to entertain that type of situation, but please remember, there is a lot of trial and error, along with much hurt, pain and drama while going through the process. Men and women truly want the same things; they just go about it in different ways. Most cases you end up meeting someone that comes from a very different background. You end up dating for a few weeks, become intimate, and you are spending a great deal of time with each other, then after six months, someone in the relationship starts showing signs of distress, the relationship is not going anywhere, it's stagnant, not developing into anything more. This is where I present those two beautiful words, standards and expectations. Did you address your standards in the beginning and set them in place, or was there just an expectation that it would turn into this fairytale of a relationship, because it looked and felt like what you wanted? When you choose to ignore the things that could ultimately save you great heartache and time, you may end up settling for something and someone less than what you should have in your life. Going back to my Grandmother and Grandfather, he told us when he first laid eyes on her, he said to her and I quote "you are going to be my wife". Back then, most men knew what they wanted and what was needed to get it, as some do now. If you are one of those men, then stand in your truth, and say what you want, and if the woman you have laid eyes on does not meet your standards you have in mind for her to be relationship worthy, you have the right to keep it moving, the same goes for the woman.

I do not want to keep repeating myself, but it cannot be said enough; do not seek out someone who has standards or expectations that you are not willing to produce yourself. Ladies and gentlemen, it won't hurt to follow this rule of thumb if you want and desire a relationship, and want to acquire it the correct way.

If you ever want to have love in your life and want it to evolve with as little issues and drama as possible, you must first know yourself and understand how you love and operate in relationships. When I used to date, I was that woman who was not afraid to announce my standards, with a certain amount of tact and finesse of course. I didn't mind letting men know, because one, it helped to weed out the riff-raff, and second, I didn't want to waste anyone's time, and I definitely didn't want my time wasted.

I would tell who ever was interested in me, exactly what kind of woman I am, and what I needed in my life. I can definitely say this, they all loved having conversations about the possibilities of a relationship, but not everyone was down for the cause, but those who were short on the conversation, I appreciated it, because they knew, and I knew a few of those conversations were deal breakers for the both of us. But I'm sure if I said, hey I'm a "go with the flow" kinda girl, or hey we are both adults, let's go have sex, if that is what we both want to do. Most men would feel that wouldn't have been too forward or too soon to ask for? They would have entertained all the above, because those situations are too easy, and no work is involved.

But it was too soon to talk about my wants and needs concerning a relationship though. Come on people; get your priorities in a straight line! How is it you are willing to risk your life by laying with a stranger, but scared to communicate your standards, morals and values to someone?

I wish everyone could come with warning labels or even disclaimers. You know how a new drug hits the market, and when the commercial comes on, they tell you all the good stuff loud and strong, then the voice gets really soft, or they speed up the words when they tell you the effects of the drug, and what will happen with prolonged use or if you have certain underlined conditions. I challenge you all to create your own disclaimers and warning labels, and if and when someone is seeking you out as a potential partner, these are the things you can discuss openly and honestly. I mean, don't just give the facts where they get awesome results if they pursue you properly, consistently, and treat you right, also give them the facts that if they make you mad, disrespect you or cheat; let them know you may cause harm and it may have an adverse effect on you and the relationship. Have fun with this. You will probably discover some things about yourself that are amazing, while discovering some other areas of your life that may need some serious attention and improvement. No one is perfect, but trust me, you are and will be perfect for someone. Sometimes we meet whom we are supposed to be with at the right appointed time and place, where you both discover that you both want and need the same things at the same time, and this becomes the relationship that overcomes many adversities that have come their way.

Timing is everything! You should be ready to welcome someone into your life if you want a relationship or marriage. Nevertheless, if you are not ready, you will surely cause chaos within your life as well as theirs and prevent something beautiful. And if you are selfish, you could care less about what damage you may cause an individual, and you decide to play the victim, when they rewind, and play your bullshit back to you. If your heart and mind is not in the right place concerning a relationship, you will cause yourself some unnecessary turmoil.

Whether you're a man or woman, if you decide to entertain a relationship or marriage and you are not ready, you will not rest easy. You will wonder why there are so many arguments, so much dishonesty and disrespect, and let us not forget about the cheating! Now, some would say cheating is cheating no matter how you look at it, and I feel those individuals without a doubt! However, I will say this, when cheating is done between two parties that are married or not married, and there are certain dynamics tied in such as, children or property, it doesn't make for an easy way out.

When you are not married, these same dynamics intertwined within the relationship, can make for a very sticky situation that could and will cause just as much heartache when someone feels

36

they have been deceived in any way. I would urge each individual who may be in these types of situations to evaluate your circumstances concerning the health of the relationship or marriage. I will never tell anyone to leave or abandon their relationship or marriage. However, if you are being abused in any form or fashion physically, mentally, emotionally or verbally, I ask you to please seek professional assistance in mending those wounds that could possibly have a lasting effect in the relationship or the next, if there is or has been long term abuse. If these situations are not dealt with, they will soon bring damage to you and possibly, your next relationship.

Most, not all men or women will endure these types of relationships and feel they are obligated to stay in fear, they may not be able to see their children, financial security may be at stake, or the fear of being on their own, alone without the assistance of their significant other. If you are dealing with someone whom you feel will cause you a great deal of unnecessary drama, grief, or pain if, or when you decide to leave, think of the same if you stay! In order for peace to be a part of this process, you must first, deal with an individual that is mentally and emotionally stable. Not saying that all people become unbalanced in high stress relationships, because some do. However, signs are shown early in the beginning of a relationship that should have been attended to. What a person may be capable of saying or doing to cause hurt or harm to a degree they may become unhinged in a relationship, is toxic. If you are already in this type of situation, in order to take the necessary precautions, you will need to do the following to protect yourself or others; as much as I deter bringing them in, you will need to seek legal advice, and maybe even deal with the police department, or courts for your own protection. Some folks do not think you are serious until you bring in the authorities. The fact is that some don't want to take you seriously, because they feel or think you will not follow-through on taking these types of measures to protect yourself or others. Please do not attempt to take matters into your hands, because you think you know them, and can talk to them and calm them down. You cannot reason with those that are, or may be disconnected from reality, or those that may have been hurt beyond the point of reconciliation.

I am sure a few of you know this situation intensifies when you have moved on to another relationship or marriage, and the other party has not moved on in their own life. Someone may still be stuck in his or her feelings and/or emotions from past hurts or pain from the previous relationship. The truth is, most men do not need closure, however, some women feel they do, and will seek it out by all necessary means; even if it interferes with your current relationship.

If you do not follow through with handling your business to seek peace for yourself, you will forever be on the rat wheel of unresolved issues when it comes to past relationships or life period. Be true to your word, and mean what you say. You cannot be this person, who is so in denial, and worried about the other person's feelings, wants or needs, when they are obviously not even considering yours. No, this is not being unkind at all; this is being someone who does things in decency and in order, with purpose to protect your heart, mind, body and spirit. It's just sad that people will play on your kindness and the fact that you have a big heart, because they know that you are such a caring individual and if the person who is sowing so much discord, shows a little act right, that you will not follow through with reporting them to the authorities. Please know that manipulators can easily identify those that are naïve or desperate and want to be free from conflict. You have to maintain a certain amount of confidence in yourself in order to stand up to these types of situations. Do not allow yourself to fall prey to such situations that do not produce the best outcomes, but if you were the one that planted those bad seeds, then you shall reap the fruits of that labor! For every choice and decision, there are consequences and repercussions. Make good choices and not just in your best interest but in the best interest of the individual that could potentially affect your life, however, good bad or indifferent.

Chapter 4

Don't Lose Yourself in Compromise

By: Anthony Branch

In life, we must understand there are different degrees of love. You do not love your pets, as you love your children, or love any of your friends; as you love your parents, etc. A lot of people throw the word LOVE around, like it's a beach ball that children play with at the beach, that obviously has no emotional attachment with it; but it's cool to say at that particular time I guess (especially men). Some men tend to tell women what they want to hear, instead of how they really feel. Women will also do the same thing as men, but not as much, women are more attentive to their real feelings than men, because men are more calculative and logical with their personal feelings.

Some individuals will tell their next possible mate/partner, the things that they think they want to hear, because they want to be what their possible mate/partner is looking for; but the sad part is that you can't be all things to all people.

Most successful couples that I personally know (or know of), are not everything to their mates; because no individual and or couple are perfect. There are differences in all of us that makes us unique (positively or negatively), because deep down inside, we all like a little challenge. That's why you hear stuff like "Opposites Attract", because most people don't date people like themselves; because they really know their own flaws deep down inside.

Trying to love another person who maybe a little different than you are, is definitely a "Chess Game"; and in some other cases "Russian Roulette". Love will be the hardest thing in your life, which you will have to truly try to figure out; because it's relative to each individual separately.

Some individuals will eventually "Compromise or Sacrifice" themselves, to try to get the things we need out of other people like Love; but we shouldn't have to do so if this thing called LOVE Is REAL.

Like I previously stated Love can be complicated, but true love is always worth it; because true unconditional love is really rare today; but possible with the correct mindset and expectations.

I honestly feel some people get "Compromise and Sacrifice" mixed up, but here is my personal take on it.

If you have to Compromise yourself to the point, where you disappear in the relationship, and you are really not yourself, is that relationship really worth it? Remember a relationship like that is not healthy for you, it will basically just stroke the other person's ego; but not in a positive way.

I think we should only "Sacrifice" ourselves for our children and parents, because at the end of the day the other person can leave; but your children and parents will always carry these titles/positions in your life. Yes, there are certain sacrifices that should be made concerning relationships, only if both are willing. This cannot and should not be one-sided. Children grow and go on, and parents, will soon pass on. However, your spouse or significant other is there for the long haul to do the ground work not meant for the responsibility of our children or parents Remember what they used to say, "Love Don't Love Nobody", but neither will a fool who is ego driven and trying to control your emotions; with that word called LOVE.

So Please be careful when you start doing all this "Compromising and Sacrificing", to gain or stay in a relationship, and it is okay to move on; stop staying in relationships that are toxic to you mentally.

"STOP THINKING BEING SINGLE TODAY IS A BAD WORD, OR THINKING YOU ARE A FAILURE IN LOVE; TIME & PATIENCE WILL EVENTUALLY BRING YOU YOUR SPECIAL PERSON".

Chapter 5

Stop Being Ego Driven

By: Anthony Branch

As we mature in our lives, we again tend to put expectations on ourselves, some unreasonable; while others are very achievable. One thing we all must admit to ourselves (if you're being real with yourself), you have an "Ego"; we all do.

Some individual's "Egos" are very inflated, while others are somewhat "Low Key".
We all think of ourselves "Higher" than we are willing to admit to, but that's understandable; unless you have "Low Self Esteem".

My personal problem is with the ones, whose "Egos" drive them to the point of being "Ugly", which will destroy a relationship;

because it's all about them (Compromising isn't a part of their vocabulary). We all have certain things in life we will do or will not do; that "Ego Driven People" will expect you to do what they do (in their minds they think they know better than you all the time). An "Ego Driven Person" will try to shoot you down or belittle you, once they realize they can't flip you or your opinion of a specific thing or person.

We all know someone like this, unless that someone is you.

Please make sure you understand the issues or possible faults in your mate, and know that we all have a limit on what we will "Tolerate"; from any relationship.

Love is a "beautiful thing", but love takes work, love is an "Action Word"; like a flower that constantly needs water to truly blossom. You must give love what it needs, so that both of you can receive nourishment from it; or that love won't be a healthy one.

We all are responsible for keeping our individual egos in check, because if not, arguments will become a part of your daily norm; and no one really wants to deal with that (hopefully).

I know my faults, and the things that will trigger my ego to take over (negatively); so, I try to personally stay away from conversations or people that might take me there. Things you have issues with in your relationships, should be treated the same way, a happy medium must be found in the relationship; so that the relationship can continue to exist.

Never let yourself get or be so big in your relationship, where you drown the other person; give a place or space in the relationship where they can breathe.

When you or your mate actually cross the line, apologize quickly; don't wait until feelings and attitudes are way beyond the "Forgiveness State". You know what I mean, no speaking to one another, sleeping in separate beds/areas of the home; or the "Rolling Of The Eyes" at one another.

No matter what happens in or during these times, try to be an Adult about it; because that's probably your only saving grace at this point.

Those couples who are married or not, that master these areas on conflict or disagreement, will survive this adversity; and come out better on the other side of it.

Those individuals, who don't handle this situation or area well, have to seriously sit down and discuss their future together; because this will definitely be a pivotal moment in the relationship. Love can be many things to many people, but love is definitely not one this, "Kind"; if the two adults leave this relationship "Bitter". Again, stay Adults about it, even if things don't work out between you two, and remember life isn't over; and will go on regardless.

Chapter 6

Be Honest About What You Want

By: Anthony Branch

When we know the new relationship is starting to become a serious one, be honest with your significant other and yourself; about things within the relationship. Some individuals will "Fake The Funk" on you, by telling you what they think you want to hear, but it's not really the whole truth; from what they probably have said to you previously. It's never too early to state your expectations, on how you would like the relationship to go, at least the other person will know (early enough) where they stand, and know if this new relationship is worth fighting for; because you'll hate to find out later that you have wasted your time.

Be very careful about this thing called "Honesty", some individuals claim they want it in their lives; and then have problems handling it once they get it. Remember a lot of people don't think like you do, so naturally their answers or behavior to situations might just throw you off your game for a little bit. Remember every new relationship is a challenge, be it good or bad; the relationship will go where you direct it. Never be afraid to be that "Traffic Cop", because successful relationships just don't happen; they are "Molded/Made".

I personally love to see couples/marriages that have navigated themselves, through the relationship "Minefields"; that sometimes blow up in other's faces.

True love is such a beautiful thing, so we need to stop putting chains on each other (Emotionally), love is love; we make it difficult to simply love one another.

We are not meant to be alone; we are really social type of beings; so sometimes we must let nature take its course etc.

If you are lucky enough to find that person, that your heart desires, don't be afraid to "Dive In" and take a chance. Life is so much better, when you are able to share it with another; especially someone that you have feelings for.

The readers of a book like this are older/mature, so we shouldn't be out there dating to be dating; it should be with the intent to build some kind of future together.

Remember a successful relationship is crafted and built to last, beyond them many storms of life, that will come your way; so, building a strong foundation is a must (A Building Built On A Weak Foundation Can't Stand For Long). Honesty is the basis of any good or strong relationship, which will also branch out to other positive things in your life.

Stay away from any kind of "Deception" in your life, because nothing positive will ever come from it; and the loss of Relationships and Friends could be devastating.

Once you can't be trusted by the individuals who know you, the chances are you definitely won't be trusted by those who really don't; because rumors of one's lies or deceptions always seem to travel fast. So, I believe in HONESTY, even when it could hurt me personally; because the truth is the truth.

We as individuals should expect "Honesty" from others, like family, friends or strangers but remember you must also give it in return.

Honesty is a beautiful thing, but you must handle "Honesty" with care; because "Honesty" can be dangerous (think about it). Some individuals would rather deal with a lie, than the "Honest Truth"; reality can be hard to deal with if you're not ready for it.

You probably won't get the truth all the time from certain people, but you don't lower your expectations or standards; because others don't have integrity or character.

Karma is real, and it will catch up with individuals who are not truthful; it always does in time.

Chapter 7

The Completion

She said, He said

In this last and final chapter, we were given a series of questions where the public needed some clarity concerning these particular views. We were able to give answers to each question from a man and woman's perspective. We both took the time to answer as honestly as possible with an open mind, and with as much information to give you a true sense of how men and women think the same or differently. You will be able to see and use what works for you, concerning the guidance given from a man and woman's perspective. If we learn how to fight fair, meaning "stop bringing a gun to a knife fight" and learn how to disagree while still obtaining some type of resolution, we will surely see ourselves on the path to healthy relationships.

1. **What makes a good or long-lasting relationship? Is it common goals, values or interests?**

She Said

To acquire a meaningful and lasting relationship, you need all of these components, and you must take inventory of yourself, know who you are, and be happy and consistent with wanting to become a better version of yourself. If you find yourself putting on another face in the presence of others, you may want to reconsider entertaining a relationship until you put these inconsistent personalities in check. Wanting a meaningful and lasting relationship is a state of mind and something both people must want, and not for a moment or until something better comes along. Even though we are different people coming into the relationship, there must be some key factors that pull us in the same direction for us to even establish a conversation or connection. We can have common goals, interests and values, and still miss the mark when seeking a mate. Open communication from both individuals is vital, while listening is a key ingredient; we must want to hear and adhere to each other's needs and requests. If you know in your heart that you are not capable of meeting the requests and /or needs of your prospective partner, please communicate this to prevent time being wasted. Some will still jump into a relationship head first knowing they do not check any of the boxes that will position them to be in a committed relationship. Most people will think; if they get with him or her, they can change them to what they want them to be. Some will charm their way through, by lying and manipulating, or they feel someone will accept their foolish and selfish ways, because it is foolish and selfish thinking if you try getting involved with someone, and you are not on their level emotionally, mentally, or spiritually. I would hope, as we are getting older and seeking relationships, that we are approaching them as whole individuals, if not you will become a settler, or a perpetrator. Settlers are those who will take what they can get and try to be comfortable and content in it, yet they are completely miserable and will find any and every little thing to cheat! I've seen this situation with more women than men. Some women would rather settle for having half a man, than no man at all! However, some men can and will fall into this situation as well. You will accept a person, married, or in multiple relationships or situations, be completely disrespectful and treat you less than your worth, but because he or she is so attractive or great in bed, you hang onto their every word, like its gold, and they can do no wrong. You don't even realize that their looks and bedroom action could be a huge deflection, because they have nothing else to offer. Anybody can give you some conversation, but not everybody will give you conversation with substance. You have those men and women out there who talk in circles, about the same thing over and over again; adding nothing of value to you or the conversation.

As far as someone perpetrating a big ole fraud, you can only do this but for so long and it will soon come to an end. The issue I have with situations such as this is, we get upset when the person shows us who they really are, and the person who's the perpetrator suddenly plays the victim. The truth is, in some instances the perpetrator shows their true-self little by little, and you will sometimes miss it because you may be caught up in the hype; the money hype, he showing you off to his friends and family hype, the sex hype, the bedroom and pillow talk hype.

No one is perfect, but you can and will find what is perfect for you! I am sure you have heard the phrase; "you will never find someone who will be everything you want and need", and usually the one saying that is still looking for love, or have settled for what he or she could get or got. I am not judging you if you did choose to settle for someone who didn't check all of your boxes. However, you choose not to go any further in your quest for love; you may have been all right with him or her not checking all your boxes and you were good with the odds that the situation presented. Just remember, this is your life and if you are tired of waiting for the right one to come along you will become desperate and lazy in your choices and decision-making when it comes to choosing your life partner.

When seeking someone to spend your life with, you would like to have someone with some of the same common interests, goals, morals and values. However, it does not always happen this way. Sometimes you get caught up in the things that physically attracted you first, and it wasn't his or her morals or values! Let's just be honest, we all want someone that we are attracted to physically. You still need to do a little more digging to see if this person is even worth your time. Let's not forget, after you throw your morals and values out the window, and you hopped straight in the bed, now you have totally missed the opportunity to find out what he or she could add to you other than some wet sheets. It is situations such as these that make some men and women sluggish in doing the ground work to truly seek someone of substance. I will end the answers to these questions with this; if you know you have nothing to add to the man or woman you are pursuing, you may want to rethink a few things, because it will be over before you actually ever began. The situation will become stale and stagnant with most of the conversations beginning or ending awkwardly, it will feel forced and uncomfortable. Do not begin anything on a shallow foundation.

He Said:

Communication, Communication, Communication... Trust is obviously a part of that communication, along with the positions each individual role is in the dynamics of their relationship. Remember no two relationships are exactly alike, so please stop comparing; because there is no real perfect relationship (all are a work in progress).

2. Biblically, when is it ok to divorce or leave a marriage?

She Said:

God declares in Malachi 2:16 *"I hate divorce"*. Why, you ask? Because God designed and ordained marriage. The first relationship God created was the covenant of marriage. Marriage was not meant to be broken by any man including the one that said, "I do". Divorce is permitted in the bible but it is not encouraged. There are only a few reasons in the Bible that releases an individual from marriage such as sexual infidelity, but you are not supposed to remarry if your current spouse is still living. However, if you are a believer married to an unbeliever, and the unbeliever chooses to divorce or leave the marriage, you are no long bounded by marriage. God has called us to live in peace. *I Corinthians 7:12-15*

Listening and waiting on God to lead and direct our path takes one to have a relationship with the Father. Sadly, we tend only to listen to Him when we are in turmoil or feeling broken. God intends for us to be whole individuals.

When it comes to "relationships" God needs to be in the midst of it all, if there is no spiritual connection with the person you desire a

relationship or marriage with, it will only be just that a
RELATIONSHIP OR MARRIAGE with no purpose headed
nowhere!

God gives us free will! Free will to do what we desire. Some
people feel that all marriages are ordained by God; not so. Most
marriages and relationships, God did not even put together. God
probably wasn't even a part of the planning of the wedding or
relationship in the first place. We choose our own mates. When
God is in the midst of a relationship or marriage, you should be
able to identify the plan and purpose for its coming together. If
there is no plan or purpose, how can you think God is the cause of
the union! When referencing marriage, let us go back to Genesis
when God purposed woman for man! He put Adam to sleep and
created the woman out of man. God desires to be in the center of
all things concerning man. This was, and still is the original plan
for marriage. However, we complicate marriage, and the things it
takes to build a strong foundation to preserve it, but will simplify
the process by dissolving it.

When we purpose things for ourselves and leave God out, we tend
to go in the direction of those things that bind us by history or
comfort. Our happiness comes from within, and the company we
keep will either build us, break us, stagger us or fulfill us. The
reality is YOU KNOW WHEN SOMETHING IS, AND WHEN
SOMETHING AIN'T! When you accept the advance of one's

request to get married, or divorce, what is the purpose behind either request and will you have peace in your decision? When someone is broken, God is who makes us whole. When you have a true relationship with God you will know His voice and seek His presence, and you know when His Spirit is leading and guiding you. Do not mistake those things that are familiar to be of God, or think that is what God has for you. When an individual is not whole, you could possibly be drained mentally, emotionally, physically, and definitely spiritually by their words and deeds. Be not deceived!

When you meet someone, there are so many components that generate what we call a prelude to a relationship or marriage. Because you marry an individual, it is not always of God. In some instances, you marry a person whose intentions and motives were all wrong for you and the marriage. You should not allow a marriage or relationship to be one of convenience or co–dependency. Both should have the same agenda and purpose for the relationship.

There should be several things that should draw your relationships together; here are a few components that I feel are very vital to the introduction of relationship needed for development:

Spiritual Chemistry

Chemistry Energy

Mental Chemistry

Emotional Chemistry

A look, a touch and sometimes a word can develop into purpose and connections for individuals to come together. Sometimes we think it's love at first sight but in actuality, it's two souls connecting with the same things that God has purposed. Our spirits are to connect first and foremost! When you undoubtedly know what your purpose is for a relationship, you may become attracted to someone with the same purpose and plan in mind, this is when you know that it is God's Divine Order that the two individual spirits that were whole have meshed.

Please keep this in mind; man purposed dating, not God! God's purpose and plan for man to be with woman was instantaneous. This also may be why some connections are quicker than others, and to truly know if it is of God, you need to have a relationship with God in order to hear a divine confirmation concerning being equally yoked.

God is not a God of confusion, He is a God of purpose and precision, He does all things with a plan in mind!

I will never debate anything that's in the "The Bible", but I have no problem giving my personal take on this topic/question.

I honestly feel when things get so bad, you can't even come up with fake reasons to stay. Physical and Mental Abuse is a big "No No" in my book, but some marriages do eventually run their course. We would like to think all marriages would last forever, but we all know they do not; that's why we cherish those that do achieve 40 years or more status.

Americans lead the world in divorce, and I think most people are not ready for marriage; that actually enter in them (especially some of the younger couples).

We are social beings, and feel the need to have that special person in our lives; but being selective is the key.

True love is really hard to find these days, but you must love you more, and protect your heart and sanity from the "Players"; that maybe swimming in your immediate circle like a shark.

3. Why do men cheat after getting married? Why does a man need more than one woman?

She Said:

The simple answer to this question is; if that is what a man wants to do, he will do it! A man does not have to have a reason to cheat; neither does a woman for that matter. However, most women will admit to having a reason for being unfaithful. I am not a man, so I can only speak of my experience and the several questions that I have asked men who have gone down the road of infidelity. None of them had a real basis for cheating. I can say, the majority of men did admit they were not done playing the field and still had a desire to be with other women even though they were supposed to be in a committed relationship. I also asked did they use protection, and only two (2) of the 25 admitted they used protection. So not only were they unfaithful in the relationship, they were careless in the act. This definitely concerned me. Being a woman, and knowing that men have no idea the amount of diseases that are carried from one partner to another where they will not experience having any symptoms is ridiculous! I am not judging anyone for having multiple partners; just make sure you protect yourself. Folks are having consensual sex as young as 10 years old up to 70 years old, and you can still catch whatever diseases are out there. Some feel if I keep the same partner, I am good, but you don't know who they are having sex with and you bring that mess right back home to your spouse or significant other. Now a man wanting and having multiple partners has nothing to do with anything other than ego. The wrong choices men make concerning having a revolving door of women will only come with wisdom and maturity. Some men are a little more disciplined than others. There are still a few men out there who are very selective in who they chose to have sex with, but please remember the one who you may be selective about, may not be selective about their choices concerning sexual partners. Sex is still a gamble, until you make clear choices about being with one partner. Here is the BIGGEST REASON MEN CHEAT; some men keep entertaining relationships with someone you are not compatible with in the bedroom. You need to choose someone who likes what you like, and wants what you want in the bedroom, marry that! Don't marry Laura Ingles if you know you want a Vanessa Del Rio in the bedroom! Let me be clear, you can have the total package if you in fact know yourself. Stop dating and associating yourself with persons you know mean you no good. If they do not fit your character or assist in shaping you mentally or emotionally for the better, then stop wasting your time and theirs!

He Said:

First of all, let's get this out of the way, it is more than sex in a lot of cases; it's more about having something different that's not you (let me explain).

It may initially start out as something physical, but grows into something that's not so superficial; the other person allows him or her to remove themselves away from their everyday grind. Someone different to talk to, and is a listening ear (like a bar tender); where there is no judgment or financial responsibility etc.

Some cheating situations get a little bit more serious than others, where the other person is more fun to be around than the person they are married to. So, we must ask ourselves, why; and what is she doing to keep the interest of the cheating spouse?

You know what they say, "Whatever it took to get that person; is what you need to do to keep them". The daily grind of life and work, often take you both away from "Quality Time"; date nights and romantic evenings etc.

Now you also know we have them individuals, who think they are God's Gift To The World; and see nothing wrong with their actions. These types of individuals must be avoided at all cost, because they rarely ever change; and their character flaw is their problem (not yours). The problem with individuals like these is, they can always find willing victims; to partake in their madness (for at least a little while).

4. Why does intimacy seem to diminish once the relationship is established?

She Said:

Let's face it, life happens after marriage, kids, maybe death of a loved one, depressions, financial woes, and many more situations that could bring on a pause in the bedroom, especially if you are entertaining more than one sexual partner. If and when you come into a relationship, it's beautiful, fresh, fun, and new. You and your partner should have had conversations concerning your needs as far as intimacy is concerned. We are all adults; you should not be having sex with anyone if you cannot communicate your sexual wants and needs. Let me back it up a minute, now there is a time and place to do this. However, it should not be a lead into the bedroom. It should definitely be more than one conversation, unless you are only going to engage in one sexual encounter with that individual, and that is your choice. Some men and women may have this conversation early on before getting into anything serious, if both feel comfortable in doing so, but if the both of you are not on the same page about having a conversation about intimacy wants, needs, and desires then do not push the envelope. Giving each other time enough to discover more about each other before having that talk would be in everyone's best interest.

Relationships that are based on sex sometimes fizzle faster than others, because that was the foundation. Once you have explored everything sexually with this person, you see there is nothing more to who they are, or see they have nothing else to offer you or the relationship. They were only satisfying one particular need that may have clouded your judgement, when you thought more was going to develop. I am sure there are more relationships that start out based on sex rather than substance. I urge each of you to have a conversation with yourself about what is a priority to you in a relationship, and let that be the focal point of your future conversation. If you find that the majority of your conversations are revolving around sex and intimacy, you may need to seek some professional therapy, because you may have some issues or potential issues concerning the subject.

He Said:

When a relationship is brand new, you can never get enough of it; and the intimacy is HOT. In time the Hotness tends to fade, because obviously the newness is gone; and the Hotness Has Cooled Off. Remember it takes two individuals to Tango, so it's the responsibility of both individuals to keep it New and Hot; teamwork doesn't stop at the bedroom door.

Please don't let the everyday grind of life, cause you to sacrifice those special moments with your significant other; "Teamwork Makes The Dream Work" (John Maxwell).

5. **Why do men and women tell their personal business to the person, they are cheating with?**

She Said:

First, let us look at the reasons why some men and women are unfaithful. If you were caught cheating or gave your partner reasons to think you are being unfaithful, most conversations will begin and end with a "side-eye" and argument. If there is already distrust in the relationship, most if not all conversations will lead to an argument, sarcastic remarks, disrespectful tones and everything else you could possibly think of that will have you both stagnant in the relationship. Instead of investing that time, energy and focus on the true relationship at hand, you will find yourself investing in someone and something that will yea and amen your every word. Whomever you are cheating with is not with you 24 hours, seven (7) days a week, and all of your complaints about the other person are one-sided. The person you are cheating with, you can talk to with ease, no arguing, you can lie without being questioned and nine times out of ten they will believe everything you say to keep getting their needs met physically, mentally, emotionally or financially. I have heard of the side-chic, and side dudes, but the "side-friend" really, there is no need to add someone in who will bring more chaos into your life if the sole reason of them even being there was to fulfill a sexual, emotional, mental or financial need. Yes, sure you make them your personal psychiatrist however, if the person you are cheating with really wants to be with you, because they understand you so much better than the person you are currently with, then what's standing in the way? Please don't say marriage, family, or kids; you have already jeopardized and compromised that, so save the excuses. If the both of you are so in tune with each other, then make it official. Statistically, 35% of the 50% that are married, is with a partner that has been an unfaithful, so you have a 25% chance of them not cheating on you with someone! Sometimes the person you are cheating with is ready to sacrifice or give up what they have going on to be with you. Please rethink that side-business; it may cost you more than you think! Normally, the person who someone is cheating with is single. Their life may not be as complicated as yours, and they may choose to keep it that way. They may like their freedom to see whomever they want, go and come as they please without answering to anyone, including you. They may seem so intriguing and mysterious and will probably represent all the things the person cheating wants and need from the person they are in the current marriage or relationship with. Remember why it started, and what the initial foundation was that started the affair. Sometimes you may fall right back to someone who may be familiar, an ex-girlfriend or boyfriend, sometimes even ex-husbands or wives become stars in this movie. You made them an

EX for a reason, but you undoubtedly turned to someone from the past, because you felt this was a safer way to go. It's nice to think that while you are cheating, you are telling all of your business in confidence, but the sad truth is, not all but most, will share your business with someone outside of the cheating relationship as well, so please be mindful and careful with what you share about your significant other.

They obviously got that comfortable with the other person, and got ok venting to them about their problems or concerns; looking for confirmation or solutions to them all.

No, it's not right, but that doesn't mean it is not happening; especially when there is no real communication going on inside the shared home.

This can open up the doors to other problems, especially if the other person wants to be more than the 3rd person; because they will use these complaints of your venting to their advantage.

Fix your problems at home with your significant other; taking it outside the home is risky, and will create more problems and headaches. Don't give up your love and future, over something cute and temporary; because you will find yourself alone when the dust finally clears.

Seek counseling if things start to get that bad at home, don't give up on the process or yourself; but most of all on the other person. Remember you made them #1 in your life for a reason, and whatever that reason is, don't you dare forget it, whenever you are feeling weak.

6. How do you maintain a healthy dating life after 40 plus?

Webster's definition of "healthy" is..." beneficial to one's physical, mental, or emotional state; conducive to or associated with good health or reduced risk of disease; evincing good health"

She Said:

In this day and time, many are dating after 40, and finding it very difficult to weed through the riff-raff. If you are just coming out of a relationship or marriage that you were in for a long period of time, you may not know all the ins and outs of how to get back in the dating game. I have seen more men who were married for a significant time, and once they got out of that marriage, they may feel like they have an "S" on their chest, and want to play the field with a number of women. On the other hand, some men want to anxiously find a wife ASAP, because they are used to having someone in their life, or they may have some underlined health conditions and choose not to share those, in fear of dying alone. Others will just put a ring on it, and hope they make it down the aisle before something is discovered in that regard. Past relationships that were not so great, may have left a sour taste in the mouths of many men, and they say "to hell with marriage again" or go the safe way, and choose to have a "Friend" and date them to death and string them along for the rest of their years while separated, yet still married. I have even seen where some women may deal with the same scenario with the same mindset. However, if they are over 40 and still have young children in the house, they may take a break from seeking a relationship and focus on re-establishing those relationships within the household. Nonetheless, you decide to incorporate a dating life while mothering, keep in mind a few things; if your children have already experienced seeing unhealthy and/or toxic relationships in your past, what will now be the standard? What will you do differently?

First things first, ladies and gentlemen, please do not let your kids pick and choose who you decide to engage in a relationship with. I hope that after reading this book you will have a better understanding on how to change up the dating and relationship norms you were all so familiar with. Your children are just that, your children; if they see you are in a place to make better choices and decisions concerning your life, they will trust your judgement, not just in reference to who you chose to date and invite in your life, but also in everyday life situations. Children cannot trust your judgement if you are making senseless and foolish choices for yourself. Children have no place in your dating affairs. If you are allowing such situations to take place, you are giving room for them to pass judgement, make assessments, or even give you advice. Who is living your life? Who is the adult? If you want any chance of someone meaningful coming into your life, get your house in order, and your children under control. If your house is not right, and I don't just mean the one made of brick and mortar, but your physical being, the mental and emotional house, your heart, mind, and spiritual house. If those are not in the right place, you are not ready to introduce yourself to no one, especially to your children! After 40 you should you have set some standards in place, and you should definitely know what you want in life. Being indecisive is very unattractive, and leaves room for careless and impulsive decision-making. You are at an age that whatever relational mistakes you have made in the past should have been teachable moments for you, and the types of persons you have engaged with in past relationships should have you looking at future relationships with a completely different lens, hopefully one of clarity. If you are still struggling with not achieving all of your life's goals; such as, you are not making the kind of money you should be making, you are not living in the big house you wanted, or your wall is not decorated with a gazillion certificates or degrees, then you will carry those same insecurities into a new relationship. Having low self-confidence or self-esteem, make for bad relationship decisions. You are 40-plus, life happens to the best of us. You could have gone through a rough stage in life that may have accounted for a few of those not-so-perfect moments you are currently experiencing at this time in your life. If you decide to get to know someone long enough to have a conversation that leads to a date, and they discover in your conversation that you had some situations that hit you a little hard, and you are still recovering from those storms, they may decide, that it's a bit much for them and become disinterested. Do not get discouraged.

They can make choices and decisions about whom they may want to allow in their lives just like you. They may have come through a rough stretch themselves, and now want the freedom of not dealing with a similar situation like that again. They may already have an idea of what kind of person they need in order to move to the next step in the dating stage. Keep being honest about who you are and who you are becoming, and what you need and want in your next relationship, and you will strike the right person's interest.

Here is a small eye-opening statement from one of the many people we asked about this topic. Ms. Annette Parker shares her thoughts on dating after 40:

As a woman over 40, continuous improvements to my spiritual, mental, and physical well-being is how I can maintain a healthy dating life. Void of inner substance, individuals position themselves for a life of sickness, i.e. low self-esteem, inferiority, and trust issues, all of which will not afford anyone a positive dating life. Your dating life will be tantamount to the ever-turning motion of a merry-go round, this is without the "merry." Additionally, we must be intentional in our selections before solidifying a dating arrangement with an individual. Have numerous conversations via cell phone or zoom before dating. You may be surprised to learn that this person is not date worthy!

Hopefully, after reading this book you will be on the path to self-assurance concerning every aspect of your life.

Realistically being 40 plus years old, I would think you have had a couple of serious relationships in your life; good or bad.

These experiences should have shown you, what is acceptable to you; or what you are willing to tolerate.

This self-evolution will directly lead you to your desired Healthy Relationship. Now the disclaimer to what I just stated above is that everything in life is not as easy as it seems; a Healthy Relationship Takes Work. You must be willing to put in the time/work, to seriously reach this desired goal; because it's not just going to happen on its own.

7. Should a man in this day and time be the provider of the household?

She Said:

Old school values have changed significantly, and so have family values. I remember when a mother could have six or more children in the home and the only person working outside the home was the father. The mother may have been home however, she made sure it was a seamless process. Dad paid the bills, took care of those essentials outside the home, cut the grass, do it yourself house projects, and may have been the disciplinarian. Mom was up before everybody. She is fixing breakfast, dressing the kids, making sure everybody is brushing their teeth, or if they are dressing properly for the weather. She may even be running down the day's events, ballet, baseball, swimming, or chorus. Depending on whether she has little ones still in diapers, she may be the neighborhood carpool. Today, the United States has the highest rate of single parent homes. If you have one parent out there trying to maintain a household with two or more children, it's very difficult; even if you are at a middle-class status. In this day and time, two parent homes need two parent incomes. The more money you make the more you spend. There are men and women in today's society that prefer the traditional household setting.

However, with a traditional family setting you may need be a little more disciplined in your spending habits. In this type of household, everyone must be on the same page concerning the dynamics of maintaining traditional family values. As I stated earlier, there are so many single women that are the head of their household, and when a man does step into the picture, she may have a difficult time letting go of some of that independence after doing the work for so long on her own. If this woman truly wants a man in her life who is willing to step in as a man who knows how to lead as a man should, by communicating what his intentions are, how he will not abandon the relationship, and he will consistently plan with a purpose to have all parties in the household's best interests at heart. I am sure there are women out there who would love an old school traditional family setting if they could afford to do so. In this day and age, financial stability plays a large part, so a two-income household is vital in order to care for a family properly. If a man truly steps up to do what is necessary to take care of the woman he wants in his life, he will do so without complaint. He will also have his finances aligned with the choice that he makes concerning supporting the household whether the woman works or not. Now, if she is a woman who still contributes to the household, both will probably see it as an addition to the family finances, with both still being able to make choices and decisions within the home. He will still see her as an asset in the home regardless of her economic status or contribution to the household.

It's relative in my opinion today, because that could be the dynamics in some couples' relationships; and not in others.

In today's society it takes two salaries to live comfortably here in America, plus who says the female in the relationship is not the financial breadwinner? Being in a serious committed relationship will always be a partnership; and the couple should determine what dynamics fits their particular situation. There is no right or wrong answer here, in my opinion on this question; just communicate with your partner your wishes or concerns about the situation.

8. How do you not allow your past hurts and pains to affect your current or future relationships?

She Said:

This is a question that so many have asked me about, and I have had so many conversations about the subject of past hurts and pains. Forgiveness is the key! Forgive yourself for allowing yourself to go through such a situation that may have left you in a place of darkness and brokenness. When you are in darkness, you can't see what's in front of you or behind you, then you let people come into your darkness and you can't show them anything! They don't even know who you really are, because you have allowed this pain to take over every part of your life to a degree that everyone you encounter is now your human band-aid. You allow them to be with you just long enough for you to heal and feel good enough to move on, so you mentally and emotionally rip them off quickly, or it may have been a situation that someone caught your feelings, so you take this band-aid off a little slower. Either way, you move on to the next situation, which again may have left you wounded, and now you are back in search of another person to give you a quick false sense of healing, when realistically, your physical wounds may be healed, however, spiritually, mentally and emotionally you are still very much in pain, bruised and broken and you may even be bleeding to death. You have to make some serious choices and decisions about what you need and want. Do you want to sincerely heal from your past hurt and pain? The first step is to remove yourself from it, and those things that continuously remind you of your wounds. You no longer need human band-aids, you need people around you who are exhibiting what you should want; strength, happiness, self-confidence, wisdom, patience, love and yes, forgiveness! These people will not let you feel sorry for yourself. No pity-parties with them around, but you have to open your heart and mind and be willing to receive what they are going to show and share with you. I believe everyone heals in his or her own time, however, much time you are willing to waste by giving someone or something that much power over your life. Not everyone who is broken wants to be fixed. Some people like to carry around those broken pieces so that others can see they are broken, looking for human band-aids, and something for the moment, or in the meanwhile so they can feel good superficially.

Simply not! You can't allow your past to affect your future. Past hurts are always going to be there, deep down in your memory, but you must break away from your past pains; so that you can give your future an honest chance to make it.

Please stop comparing your life, to other individuals' lives, because everyone's relationship dynamics are not the same; so don't be the one that destroys your new relationship.

9. After how many marriages should a person be concerned about someone's marital history?

She Said:

We will not place judgement on any one who may be in their second marriage or fifth marriage. You have some who do it for sport and others because this is what they were taught. Marriage is supposed to be between you and hopefully, someone who desires and shares the same values in life; you both love the same individually and collectively. Some men and women go through these phases that if they are not married, they are looked at like they are the ones with the problem because they are single. I know for a fact that if some of those that are currently married do a self-evaluation, they will say they wish they weren't married! No one wants to be alone, and the truth is we are built for relationships. Marriage has become a joke to so many. I believe that the purpose of why some actually follow through are some of the very reasons I mentioned earlier, money, convenience, kids, or out of desperation. I honestly believe that if you didn't get it right the first time, and you truly desire marriage and what it represents, you fight to get it right the next time it does present itself. However, if you are entertaining the same type of men or women, with the same type of issues and problems, and you have the same mindset hopping from one marriage to the next, you will continue this vicious cycle of failed relationships and marriages. I believe two individuals can meet each other and get married after a few days or months and they last with little drama or issues. I believe timing plays a huge part in these particular situations. Someone felt safe enough to let their guard down, or they met someone they felt was worthy enough to straighten up and fly right. People will move from relationship to relationship because someone was not willing to accept their warped sense of reality and direction of how they think marriage is supposed to be. They will take out whoever didn't fit in the box, and try to find someone else to fit in it, sometimes while still in their current marriage, which makes for a very messy and chaotic experience. If you are dealing with, or have dealt with such an ordeal, you may be very familiar with the outcome. Again, I will never advise anyone to leave their spouse, I think marriage is a beautiful thing when both individuals want and need the same things at the same time. If you like to party and who you date doesn't, why are you moving forward with marriage? The first time one of you presents it as a problem, it will be said "you knew how I was when we got together" just as sure as my name is Tyishua, it will be said! I just pray this book will give you some insight and guidance concerning the matter. Marry what you know you need, not so much what you want!

He Said:

Again, the dynamics of where you are in your life (and age), will determine this answer. We don't know the stories and causes of another person's marital history, but anything beyond two will raise the Red Flag for me.

Please understand that we should always look for someone to love, and to love you in return. Be careful of those individuals who fall in love, with the idea of being in love; but don't have a clue on what it takes to make it work. Love is a Beautiful Thing, but Love is work too, so prepare to roll up your sleeves and get your hands dirty in this thing called Love.

10. Should you trust an individual going into a relationship, or should that trust be earned?

She Said:

Why is it that we are so quick to say, "I can't trust him or her with my emotions, deepest thoughts and feelings"? However, you trust your life daily to total strangers every single day!

Whether you know it or not, you trust people with some of the most precious and important things in your lives with whom you may not ever have had a conversation with. You trust those that you leave your children with; whether it's at the school building, or at the sitter's. You trust others to drive their cars on the road to be just as careful as you are when you are traveling day in and day out. You have even trusted people who you have had unprotected sex with, you could have contracted an unwanted disease that you could have carried back to someone else. You travel on cruise ships, trains and airplanes.

What about when you dine out at a restaurant, you are entrusting people to fix your meals in an "A" plus kitchen. However, you have great difficulty expressing your feelings to the person close to you that you may share your life with every day! You get into a relationship and shut down from speaking your truth about how you feel, how you may be changing, growing and evolving. Not revealing your needs, standards, and expectations will cause an enormous strain on the relationship as a whole.

There is great freedom in speaking truthfully about how you feel to anyone, not just those you are in a relationship with. I understand not everything is up for discussion and, there are some things that you may want to keep to yourself. There are things that you may feel ashamed about, or be in fear of judgement or criticism. If this is the case, at some point you will need to release it! Situations such as this build unwanted stress. You allow certain issues and concerns to rule and regulate your life, and maybe even some of the decisions you make may leave you broken and confused. This makes for a very miserable life.

Stress is a silent killer. Each day you allow stress to creep into your life, you are slowly decomposing!

I get it; you shared something with someone that may have been very personal for that person's ears only, and they broke your trust by passing the information on to someone else. Do you now plan to hold in every aspect of life that you may need direction or clarity with, inside to fester, leaving you worn out emotionally and mentally? Soon you will find yourself physically broken-down if you do not find a healthy outlet. Not talking about what's mentally or emotionally going on inside of you, or relying on someone to read your mind and guess at what's nagging you is not a healthy approach either.

This is just one of life's many circumstances that has left many with a serious void, so many fails to learn how to cope with the hills and valleys of life. We have even allowed society to tell us that we are not strong enough to bare these senseless burdens, to take a pill. But the truth is that many do not have the mental or emotional capacity to manage their day to day life's issues. To truly trust others, we must first trust ourselves. Someone can honestly only be to you, what you have been to them. You know what kind of friend, spouse, or significant other you are. If you gossip, tell other people's business, please know and understand you are not exempt from the same happening to you, I don't care how nice you are. Also, if you can treat the people outside your relations better than you treat the person you are in a relationship with, this will make for a terrible relationship. You are sure to have every known negative situation take place in your relationship. Showing blatant disrespect to your significant other, speaks volumes of how you feel about yourself.

Until you can be good to yourself, and listen to others without passing judgement, accept criticism as a help not a hindrance, the same will be received by you. Some people will say "I don't have a lot of friends or I don't deal with a lot of people", and you may feel this works for you, but how? Isolating yourself from people will not help your situation. I am not saying go out there and make a plethora of friends. I am saying that when you are in the presence of people with different backgrounds, religious beliefs, professional experiences and education, you will be surprised as to how quickly you are able to share bits and pieces of your life unconsciously. The more you do this, the more comfortable you become about sharing your feelings.

Our relationships with those on the outside of our world help us to identify who we really are, and it allows us to build character and a better vocabulary. These are the very relationships that help shape us into the kind of people we chose to become. You are at a party with a few people you may know, and others you may not, and two or three are standing there discussing business. You have always been interested in starting a business, but didn't know the first step. You introduce yourself as you politely interrupt to ask questions. You may have just gained a new associate that could turn into a potential business relationship and or friend. However, if you never would have spoken up because you chose not to be "people friendly", you may be missing out on some amazing teachable moments. Sometimes you just have to step out on faith and look for opportunities to share your thoughts a little at a time; this will build trust with your mate. Share things gradually, which will give you both time to process the information relayed. Take time to seek organic associations that may assist in building your trust issues for the better. Taking the baby-steps approach may work better for you, if you are the type of person that doesn't take people at face value. You cannot ask someone to trust you, when you yourself are not trust-worthy. Leading with the disclaimer, "Don't tell anybody or this is between you and me" may be something you need to think carefully about what it is you are about to say. Is this something about you or somebody else?

Trust will and can be earned when you share with genuineness. Remember, the same attitude you have toward others, will result in others feeling the same way towards you!

He Said:

Both. Why would you enter into a relationship in the first place, if you don't have a certain amount of trust for them already? There are degrees of trust, and the other degrees of trust will be earned by your partner's actions (eventually); and by their sincere commitment to the relationship at hand.

ABOUT THE AUTHORS

Tyishua McCoy is a singer/songwriter, a Brand Ambassador for Colour U Cosmetics, Founder/CEO of 7 City Divaz, and the Nonprofit organization Build Not Break, the Host of the Tough

Talk Today Show and Co Author of the book "I Support Her, The Anthology". Mrs. McCoy is also a Certified Master Life Coach, specializing in the areas of Professional, Purpose, Goals & Success Coaching.

Tyishua has created and purposed each one of the entities that she has envisioned to assist in building and strengthening those in the community.

Mrs. McCoy currently holds a Master's Degree in Business Management. Her main objective is to make significant strides in the community by uplifting, edifying and encouraging others. She has taken the time to mentor men, women and children of all backgrounds, ages, races, and beliefs.

Tyishua was raised by a single mother, who raised her, "to treat people the way you want to be treated", especially women. She says as she watched the women in her family, and how they treated each other, it was evident that the highest level of respect was given to the eldest women, and it was imperative to do so.

"While in the midst of my own trials and turmoil of life as a teenager, I experienced homelessness, teen pregnancy, sexual assault, judicial issues as well as parents who dealt with substance abuse", she says.

She also says, "It is important that we set inspiring examples for our youth, so that their quality of life will continue to be enhanced.

I have seen so many women hurt by other women, which can and has led to gender hatred. We are on the rise for change!"

Mrs. McCoy will continue to build a platform to help people identify their weaknesses and strengths, which will allow for those in our community of all ages to fulfill their purpose in life. Knowing your self-worth will not only advance one to succeed in life, but it will allow you to have the type of self-confidence that others will admire, and will want to seek within themselves.

The vision, mission, and objectives achieved by men, women, and children will be to serve as a conduit to empower, inspire and strengthen all in the areas of their lives, spiritually, emotionally, mentally, physically, and financially.

She concludes, "This is and will continue to be my mission daily!"

My name is Anthony Lyn Branch, better known today as "Coach Tony"; here in the Midwest of America. I was born and raised in New York City, yes, the "Big Apple"; the largest city in the world.

I served 20 years and 9 days in the greatest military on the planet, the United States Armed Forces; in the US Navy. I retired out of Naval Air Station Oceana on April 30th 2000, in the great city of Virginia Beach; in the Hampton Roads Region of Virginia.

I was raised by my single mother (Mattie N. Branch), who had three children total (Kim and Larry); and I was the middle child out of the bunch. My mother had seen a lot of struggles in her lifetime, that has taught me such valuable lessons over the years; that I still live by today. My mother always wanted the best for her children, and I learned so much from her personal sacrifice; her unselfishness to share with others is a characteristic I made a major part of my adult life.

I love sports, and like engaging others in conversations about life; and how we can address making things better for us all. Every struggle or tragedy in my life, had me create a principle on how I will live; that I still practice to this day.

My mentors over the years (directly or indirectly), give me what I needed to help me navigate; through this thing called Life.
Yes, I have had my share of struggles and tragedies, but with a lot of these principles, I have survived them all.

We all know how life will constantly test our character and faith, throughout the year; but staying true to oneself is the key to one's success.

I have lived my life a certain way that has caught the eyes of individuals and organizations throughout this country. I have won some local and international praise and awards, also bringing me an Honorary Doctorate Degree in Humanitarian Studies; on top of being featured on a hit ABC Network TV Reality Show "Secret Millionaire" (with my community girls' basketball team)

I know a lot of individuals have a problem understanding me and my lifestyle, and that's ok; as long as I understand myself and my purpose in life (they will eventually catch up). I can't help it that I care so much, while others care so little. While taking so much from society, but think so little about replenishing what they have taken.

I have been blessed with the ability to understand the true meaning of the word "Service" and try to live within that understanding daily.

I have written a couple of Fundraising Books, to help pay for incoming college freshmen book fees; and purchase some laptop computers. I have also organized my own "Winter Coat Drive", to provide Winter Coats to struggling single mothers; and their children in Northwest Indiana.

We can't complain about our communities, and expect the government to fix our communities; unless we are willing to do our part, "Service".

I try to be transparent, because I personally have no hidden agendas, but to bring positivity to an individual or a situation.

A life without hope is truly not a life, it's a sad situation and we are way better than that as a society.

~ Anthony Branch

EPILOGUE

Transparency is Key

Is it possible to miss you even though we never met?
Feel a connection but never have touched your flesh?
Never made love but have nothing but love to give.
Just cause it seems too good to be true, don't mean it is.
Our kids, siblings even when there's no relation.
Souls being combined just off conversations.
Minds over time filled with thoughts of each other.
Pain that one feels is now felt together.
Some things can't be explained so why should we fight it?
Fires and desires automatically ignited.
Excited for the moment that we actually meet.
But still feels content with the times we speak.
Not clear where it's going but still enjoys the moment.
Text to the ex-just giving my condolence.
Cause what we had is dead and didn't shed a tear.
Yearning for the day for her to be his.
Thinking of what to give for anniversaries that don't exist.
Walking through the malls staring at possible gifts.
I tried to give warnings these are shades of me.
I can only be who I am, transparency is key.

~ Jay Speight

The END

www.ingramcontent.com/pod-product-compliance
Lightning Source LLC
LaVergne TN
LVHW021359080426
835508LV00020B/2358